All Scripture references taken from the KJV of the Holy Bible, unless otherwise indicated.

<u>FAILED ASSIGNMENT</u>

by Dr. Marlene Miles

Freshwater Press 2023

ISBN: 978-1-960150-92-9

Copyright 2023, Dr. Marlene Miles

All rights reserved. No part of this book may be reproduced, distributed or transmitted by any means or in any means including photocopying, recording or other electronic or mechanical methods without prior written permission of the publisher except in the case of brief publications or critical reviews.

Table of Contents

- Failed Assignment 5
- Ministry of Angels 11
- When Will It Stop? 13
- We Are Not in Kansas, *Dorothy* 26
- I Have No Idols 33
- As For Me and My House 37
- Multiple Altars 40
- Smile In Your Face 42
- Surely, He Has Rejected Me 46
- Why Is This Happening? 49
- The Assignment 52
- Be Aware 58
- IYKYK 62
- We CAN Do This 64
- I Can Do All Things 67
- Friends Are Rare 72
- Pharisees 77
- Even If A Tree 81
- Make Your Boast 86
- Say No to Woe! 88
- What This Means 92

Dear Reader.. 95

Other books by this author................................ 96

FAILED ASSIGNMENT

Freshwater Press

Failed Assignment

How many people have come against you in your life, but failed? If you start way back in kindergarten you may remember childhood bullies, but remembering them is not to recall or harbor unforgiveness, pain or hurt. But as grown-up Christians let's look back and see how God has brought us *through*.

In 7th grade, every time our paths crossed, another 7th grade girl told me she was going to beat me up. She didn't want my lunch money or that I would do her book reports. She wanted nothing, just to beat me up. For no reason. I avoided recess like the Plague, stayed in and read that year. Even though she had made herself my enemy, I had not agreed with her to make her mine. I either thought of her as a girl with some type of problem, like an anger problem, or I believed that whatever she was going through, she would get over it and she would forget me. Because I didn't make her an enemy, I never said or prayed anything evil or vengeful against her, or to her. As a matter of fact, I don't think we had ever had a conversation. My prayers at that time very juvenile--, probably a lot of breath prayers such as, *Thank You's* to God, and Now I Lay Me Down to Sleep prayers at night.

There was no boy that I was interested in, so it wasn't a fight over boys--, none of that was on my radar yet. So, I just avoided her.

I don't know if she had beefs with other kids, or not. It was just me, for some reason.

She was in my same grade, but thankfully, not my same classroom. My teacher was very strict, but when I told her about the threat and what would or could happen to me on the playground at lunchtime, she advised me to stay in the classroom. Further, I was escorted, by the teacher, to my school bus at the end of each school day, for weeks.

This was a bit more terrifying, since this girl lived about a mile from my childhood home. We lived on rural roads and 13-year-olds don't have cars, or chauffeurs, so the thought that she would come to my house lasted a few seconds the one day I thought of it.

However, I had the option to ride the bus that she rode to school, or another bus. I took the other bus all that year, for sure.

I got formally saved and baptized in church at age 13--, 7th grade. If this girl went to church, it was not the one I went to, so there was nothing that could have happened between us in Sunday School. Now I see this was the devil's first plan against me. All through school I pretty much got along with every student that I knew in my school, but not this one girl.

I had never said a cross word to that girl, she just chose me as someone to hate. By 8th grade, she had died in a car accident.

You may become aware of people who are being, or have been used by the devil, to come against you and failed. They failed because God said, No! They failed because of who and whose you are. They failed because of your prayer covering, the fire around you, and it may not have even been your own doing. It was your parents' prayers, grandma's, or other friends or relatives' prayers. It may have been your church's or pastor's prayers, if you had a real pastor. It was God's great love, His amazing Grace and mercy, saying, *touch not mine anointed*.

Do you realize that as soon as you are saved and have the Holy Spirit, you are God's **anointed**? You are anointed for good works, and God even gives you spiritual gifts and abilities to accomplish the work you should be doing in the Earth. Not just one-time things, but you have signed up for a lifetime of good works, and hopefully godly exploits.

This book is about what has happened to the people of your past since your encounters with them. It is written for your awareness, and for you to realize that God has surely dealt with those who have tried to deal with you; let this bolster your faith in God. This book is to send us reminders to be thankful for what God has done for us in our lives. It is to make sure we say, Thank You to God. It is to make sure that we do not give credit to the wrong "person" for the Grace, mercy, lovingkindness, successes, and protection that God has given us all our lives, even though we may have had near misses and close scrapes.

Plead my cause, O LORD, with them that strive with me: fight against them that fight against me.

Take hold of shield and buckler, and stand up for mine help.

Draw out also the spear, and stop the way against them that persecute me: say unto my soul, I am thy salvation.

Let them be confounded and put to shame that seek after my soul: let them be turned back and brought to confusion that devise my hurt.

(Psalm 35:1-4)

Remember, you asked, even as a kid, you called on Jesus in your own way. You did pray, it is a natural instinct for most. Yes you did ask, and God answered. Remember God answered; that is the purpose of this book. Remember God brought you out of trouble, and whether you gave a testimony in the sanctuary, or a private thank You to God, you have manners, so you did say thank You, *right*?

As you are reading this, it is not too late if you have not.

God is waiting.

Ministry of Angels

We do not ignore or deny the ministry of angels. God gives His angels charge over us to keep us in all our ways. He sends us help from the Throne. There are Angels of Protection, Angels of Blessings, and there are Warrior Angels, among others. We pray to God through Jesus Christ. We do not pray to angels, and we do not worship angels.

Are they not all ministering spirits, sent forth to minister for them who shall be heirs of salvation?

(Hebrews 1:14)

Therefore we ought to give the more earnest heed to the things which we have heard, lest at any time we should let them slip.

For if the word spoken by angels was stedfast, and every transgression and disobedience received a just recompence of reward; How shall we escape, if we neglect so great salvation; which at the first began to be spoken by the Lord, and was confirmed unto us by them that heard him; (Hebrews 2:1-3)

When Will It Stop?

Some people that you didn't even realize were trying to come against you, but they were. Some were folks that you would never have imagined would ever come against you; but they did. Probably unbeknownst to you, God afforded you angelic protection. There were things He didn't even let come into your arena; His angels blocked so many things from happening to you, often. Daily. Weekly. Monthly. All your life.

Have you said, *Thank You, Lord?*

Some things may have been covered from your physical awareness back then, or even now.

The word of God says that we have authority to tread on serpents and scorpions, and over all the power of the enemy. That is pretty awesome, we have power to tread on **ALL** the power of the enemy. That is in the Spirit. This is by no means an invitation to go get physical weapons to attack folks.

> Behold, I give unto you power to tread on serpents and scorpions, and over all the power of the enemy: and nothing shall by any means hurt you, (Luke 10:19)

Unless we can clearly see in the spirit, we may be treading on things that we don't even know we are treading on, trampling on, or yesterday we already trampled on them. Therefore, things we knocked out at the spiritual level never got a chance to reach the physical. That means that demonic plans in the spirit were defeated before they ever entered into the mind and heart of an evil human agent, knowingly or unknowingly and came up against you, in the natural.

The fact that you have, see, or know of a natural enemy means that at the spirit level this evil plan got through. It wasn't blocked in the spirit, but came into manifestation in the Earth. That either means no one saw it, no one knew of it, no one perceived it, and therefore no one prayed against it, or pulled it down as a high thing exalting itself against the knowledge and plans of God.

We can know about things and do nothing, which is not the same as not knowing about it. Knowing about it and doing nothing about it makes us guilty. To know to do and not to do it is sin to a man.

Therefore to him that knoweth to do good, and doeth it not, to him it is sin,
(James 4:17)

The Word of God is true. If God says we are able to do the above, then we are. If we are still standing, still vertical after all these years of living, surely, we have already done the above, at least once, and are likely in a position to do it again and again.

Often, referring to the trials of this life, people say if it is not *one thing* then it's the other. Well, the *one thing* comes up against you, where does it go? If it didn't take you down, or out, then it was defeated. Either you defeated it by the power and authority of God, or God did, in His Mercy.

Relieved that is is over? Yes, but have you ever thought the trial, test, or tribulation went somewhere? It was dissipated, defeated, drowned, run off --, something. It failed against you.

Okay, then the *other thing* comes up against you, have you asked yourself why? Why would another thing need to come up against you, if the *one thing* (the first thing) had already accosted you? It's because the first thing failed. **FAILED ASSIGNMENT**. The first assault the enemy sent failed, that is why he sent another, that is why he had to send another.

The first attempt was a failure: **FAILED ASSIGNMENT.**

For this we can rejoice and give God thanksgiving, praise and worship!

A steady stream of devil-influenced, devil-directed folks may be sent into your life to try to trick you, irritate you, entice you. These things have been sent against any of us. Even the evil ones will at first try to *nice* you, butter you up, bribe, entice, befriend you. They may try charm; if that doesn't work, then they resort to evil because *nice* didn't work. It is as if they get more desperate, so they use more desperate measures.

You've surely seen it more than once--, the friend who became a fake friend, or maybe always was a fake. The coworker who wasn't genuine… the sibling that you wonder if they were switched at the hospital, or if your whole family is behaving weirdly, you may wonder if ***you*** were the one who was switched at birth, because *who* are these people right now?

Seeing the truth of repeated or occasional enemy attacks is no reason to be bitter, these are facts of life and facts of people. Folks are just folks. Those with the Spirit of God should behave a certain way, and those with other *spirits* will behave other ways. Going through life, we have to be discerning so our godly purposes are not derailed, delayed, or re-directed.

As long as you are on the path of your destiny and in your purpose, you will always have the support and protection of Heaven. If you are on your destiny clock and the calendar that God has established for your life, you will be divinely protected by God. Yes, He is protecting his Plan for mankind, but you get protection as well if you are walking upright before the Lord and in obedience.

Sneak attacks and sneaky people are a devil specialty. Come on, what would-be-nemesis would say, I'm here to exchange or stop your destiny? Like the snake in the Garden at Eden, there will be subtilty – which means sneakiness, lies, deception, and enticement--, in any order that is deemed to work on you.

Yeah, but you just want it to stop. Make it stop! One or more of several things must happen to make it stop.
1. <u>You</u> stop it by prayer and spiritual warfare.
2. God stops it because it's illegal, it's too much, or because it is over.
3. God stops it because you won and have entered a season of rest.
4. It stops because you finished your course and reached destiny.

Only with thine eyes shalt thou behold And see the reward of the wicked. Because thou hast made the LORD, which is my refuge, Even the most High, thy habitation; There shall no evil befall thee, Neither shall any plague come nigh thy dwelling.

Psalm 91:8-14

God will show you the outcomes of the wicked who come up against you, if you are one of His and you seek Him, ask Him, trust Him, and let Him minister vengeance. You must stay out of the flesh and stay prayerful. As you reflect now, you may realize that God **has** shown you the reward of a lot of wicked that may have come up against you in your life, so far.

God can show you in a dream, or in the natural the destruction of the wicked that have arisen or been on assignment against you.

One night, just last month, I saw five witches die, in the dream. They were dropping like flies as they were trying to run away or get away. An angelic host descended ready for more battle, and/or protection, but five evil entities, or evil workers had already dropped dead.

I woke up before I saw the rest, or what came next, but God will show you as well. What had I been praying? My prayers were against the *powers* behind the problems that I was experiencing in life. We do not war against flesh and blood, but we pray in the Spirit against evil *spirits* and God will send help from the Throne. Amen.

I've seen strongmen defeated. One was in the street driving one of those pavement smoother machines, as if he was working on a street that had been scraped to its foundation. Really, he was trying to get away. He was struck down by a sniper on the roof of a building; that strongman lay paralyzed in the street. This was also in the spirit, in the dream state, but I had been praying to bind and paralyze the strongmen of my father's house, and of my mother's house.

We can't rest on laurels, because how do we know, until we get peace from God, how many strongmen there *are*? So, we keep praying. When I say I had been praying, I mean for weeks, months, even years before I saw the reward of the wicked. Because of and when I had that dream, that does not mean that it *just* happened, it means that's when I saw it. Further, it may not have happened yet, it could have been a prophetic dream. God will often show you things that He is about to deliver you from, and give you the victory.

The war is hot, so keep the warfare hotter, so you will be victorious. But God will show you the outcome of enemies who come against you, in the Spirit as well as those who have worked evil against you, God will show you their defeat, even in the natural. Don't war with flesh and blood. Don't set out for revenge or payback; God's got this. You keep praying in the Spirit.

In the natural, haven't you seen those against you, lose out in life? They lose jobs, they lose relationships, because they came against yours. They lose opportunities, money, health, and worse as their plans against you have backfired. There was another man who was used by the devil against me, I discussed that at length in my book, **Tormenting Spirits**. I never asked God to do anything to that man, but he is no longer alive on Earth.

God teaches the wicked with their own evil.

"I the Lord search the heart and test the mind, to give every man according to his ways, according to the fruit of his deeds." (Psalm 24:4 ESV)

God is Just, but He is not blind. God is not deaf. God is not idle. God is doing something. Even when you don't see Him, He's working. Even when you don't feel Him, He's working. God is ever working on our behalf as we live by every proceeding Word out of the mouth of God.

God is patient, longsuffering, and kind.

Sometimes God can't move on your behalf because YOU are in the way. If God steps in to punish the idol *gods* and you've made alliances, covenants, and marriages with these idol *gods* – God can't do anything short of taking you out with them.

By His Mercy, He gives you more time to repent and get it right.

We may all think these are unsaved people rising up against us. For the most part, they are, but maybe not always. We may think they are strangers, people who don't look like us, think like us--, sometimes, but not always. Depends on who and what is in their soul. The idols in a man's soul are there to influence him to do what the idol *god* wants done in the Earth, and against mankind. If that man even if he is saved, is not submitted fully to the Holy Spirit, other *spirits* can direct him to do this, that or the other.

The man who does not have the Holy Spirit is like an open vessel that *spirits* can go in and out of, at will, to make that man their puppet. And that man may never know it. That man may never know himself. He may think that he is the sum total of all the evil that visits and inhabits him and gives him evil thoughts and promptings. That man is fully captive, while demons infest and use his body in the Earth.

How you fare in life from day to day depends a lot on you. If you're saved, if you're paying attention, if you are filled with the Holy Spirit, and you pray and pray well, you will not have very much to worry about in your life. Things should go very well for you.

But if you are prayerless or careless, your protection is compromised, and so will your life be.

So, pray regularly, and pray well.

We Are Not in Kansas, *Dorothy*

Dorothy, we are not kids in Sunday school anymore. We are all living a real life, not some fantasy or fairy tale.

I woke up this morning with a Word that the Lord would not let me let go of, so I'm sharing it. We serve a God of balance.

> It is mine to avenge; I will repay.
> In due time their foot will slip;
> their day of disaster is near
> and their doom rushes upon them,
> (Deuteronomy 32:35 NIV)

We serve a God of balance,

> A false balance is abomination to the Lord: but a just weight is his delight,
> (Proverbs 11:1)

A just balance and scales are the LORD's;
all the weights in the bag are his work,
(Proverbs 16:11a)

Let's look at this warfare: Your enemy is firing evil arrows at you, and you're firing nothing, that's out of balance, that's not balanced. Your enemy is shooting a gun, and you have a BB gun--? That is also out of balance. It is an unjust balance. Your enemy is shooting an automatic weapon, but you have a fly swatter? Unjust balance--, for sure. Your enemy is firing evil arrows and you're chanting the Golden Rule?

Dorothy, we're not kids in Sunday school anymore. We serve a God of balance. God is balanced in everything. He's even counted the hairs on your head--, even the ones that are *supposed* to be there. He knows the sands in the desert, the stars in the heavenlies. **Don't you think God knows how many evil arrows the devil has and how many he's gonna have**

and where they are and who they're going to be aimed at?

And He also knows that sometimes we don't know any of that stuff. Sometimes we don't know anything because the enemy is constantly trying to hide his evil plans against us, from us.

But wouldn't God give you means and support to defend and protect yourself, your family, and all things that you have stewardship over? God does not waste; He does not pour on the ground. God would not give you things to lose or to have the devil take those things from you.

Sometimes we have to learn how to protect a thing before we GET that thing, so we can KEEP that thing. Selah.

God knows the amounts of everything, the timing of everything, and the balance of everything. In God, we are more than conquerors. We should win every time and every battle, when we seek

Him, unless we, ourselves are under judgment from God.

God knows everything, and He's a God of balance and justice. Furthermore, he is not planning that anything bad should happen to you or me. He has plans for a future for us, and he's not going to let anything happen to us.

Thank You, Lord.

God is a God of justice; He believes in justice. If we sin, the Law automatically comes into play. The Law of Sin and Death is for sinners; if we sin, that Law stands until we repent. After that, hopefully we don't sin anymore, so we don't have to be under the Law of Sin and Death.

But Jesus has redeemed us from the curse of the law, thank You, Lord.

So then, how are Sinners supposed to be rewarded for sin if <u>we</u> are not rewarded for sin? If for sin, we get *death,* how do sinners get prayers with us blessing them? This makes no sense to me; does it make sense to you? Yet, this is what we learned in Sunday school--, *Dorothy*. Bless your enemies. Mature Wisdom must be used here:

- Lord, bless my enemies, according to Scripture, but don't let them continue to hurt me, in the Name of Jesus.

Whether the sin is against us or whether it's against other sinners somehow the reward is not a blessing. Somebody fires evil arrows at you you're gonna bless them? No-- **return to sender.** If we are blessing them no matter what they do – something you wouldn't even do for a child that needs to learn discipline, that's empowering them. Blessing them when they are as wrong as dirt will embolden them, and it will keep them able to hurt you. *Is that what you really want?*

And, doing so says you **agree** with them, thus forming an ungodly alliance--, an evil alliance. God says don't do that. It's forming an evil contract; it's giving your grace away to evil and to sin and to the devil, casting pearls to swine and putting lipstick on the same. Pretty? No, ugly and stinky.

Many will argue that back to sender is seeking vengeance. Return to sender means that I am asking God for what I want. God is Sovereign, He decides what will happen with any evil arrow that I deflect with the Shield of Faith, which is a weapon of our warfare, which He gave me. God will decide what happens with any evil arrow that I dip into the Blood of Jesus and return to sender. God makes the ultimate decision on what will happen to any entity, agent, power, or person who is shooting evil arrows at His children.

David, a man after God's own heart, asked God to give his enemies hemorrhoids, among other things.

In prayer, I take the opportunity to agree with Scripture and I would be foolish not to. If you roll a stone, it will roll back on you. People fall into pits that they dig for others. God teaches the wicked by their own wickedness.

> The righteousness of the blameless makes their paths straight, but the wicked are brought down by their own wickedness,
> (Proverbs 11:5)

If I am a soldier in the army of the Lord, then I do soldier stuff, which means I use weapons. I am not naming any individual in the return to sender prayer, I may not even *know* who, in the natural, sent it, but I am warring against spiritual wickedness and powers in high places as instructed in Ephesians 6.

You do as you will. But as for me, since My God is a God of War, the Lord is His name, when He says, or when indicated, I will war.

I Have No Idols

Of course, you don't have any idols, no idol *gods* --, but you really do. No curse can alight without a cause, so nothing ungodly could EVER happen to you, unless there is a place in you for an *idol* to latch onto. That means, as <u>we all</u> have sinned and fallen short of the glory of God, like dirt, germs, bacteria, and the like, we have picked up idol *gods* because they want to be with us and where we are, and we may not even be aware that we've collected any.

Or worse, that *they* have collected us.

So, stuff is happening to you because the idol *gods* that you are in relationship with want **worship** and you are either not giving them enough worship, or you've stopped completely because you are now saved. You are saved, but these idols are behaving as though they didn't get the memo or pretending that they didn't get it. So, the *idols'* language of YOU OWE ME, is sending punishments into your life to hurt you for not giving what they believe is theirs.

Sometimes those punishments can be torment, sabotage, losses, disappointments, and hurts --, **through humans**. The humans are those who come into your life to mock you, interfere with work, or relationships, money, health, peace, joy, or to torment, threaten, or beat you up--, sometimes for no apparent reason.

Read this well, some of the nice, friendly ones entice you into sin, which if you fall for, now you have renewed the contract that had either expired because you did accept Christ as your Lord and Savior, so now they have a way, again, to enter into your life to jack it up by stealing, killing and destroying.

If you don't fall for the *sinvitations* (my word), then that file will be stamped against the enemy of God and also your enemy: **FAILED ASSIGNMENT.**

Congratulations to you! Amen.

That was one. One down, or another one bites the dust; however, the devil has a lot of potato chips in his bag to tempt a man.

You may be saying, *I thought that if I get saved and submit myself to God, and resist the devil that he will flee from me.*

Yeah, that's what the Word says. But have you really submitted fully to Jesus? Are you really resisting the devil?

Doing everything you've always done and adding church to your routine on Sunday and/or one night a week is **not** all that is involved in resisting the devil.

Better put, one should resist the WORLD. There, that makes better sense, doesn't it?

Love not the world, neither the things that are in the world. If any man love the world, the love of the Father is not in him.

For all that is in the world, the lust of the flesh, and the lust of the eyes, and the pride of life, is not of the Father, but is of the world.

And the world passeth away, and the lust thereof: but he that doeth the will of God abideth for ever. (1 John 2:15-17)

Wait a minute! If I do all that, I won't have any fun. Hell is not fun, but it is eternal. Choose ye this day, life or death. Are the temporal pleasures of this world enough to sway you? The devil asks that question of humans every day, all day and all night, as he sends *one thing*, and if that fails, he sends *the other*. Do not choose the world. Do not be in love with the world; people a subject to hell for that. Don't let that be you.

As For Me and My House

Like father like son – the idols of your father's house are looking for you. The idol *gods* your father served, are looking for you. Constantly.

Unless you are saved, accepted Jesus for yourself, and you have renounced these *idols*, you are automatically expected to follow them. Often, you **are** already following them because what's in your blood, calls to you. Who does every little boy want to be like? His dad. And every little girl? Her mom. Usually. So, if dad wears a cap on his head every day, you will either choose to do that, or will find yourself doing it.

It's why after a certain age we can look in the mirror and see our parents looking back at us, even if we swore that would never be the case. (Don't swear.)

Sin is by invitation, **sinvitations** are coming at you 24/7, and because of your blood, you automatically <u>like</u> those things; you automatically <u>want</u> those things. You don't know why, it just somehow makes sense to you, or you think it will be fun, or that it will satisfy you.

Your momma could even ask you, *Why did you do that?*

You do not know.

It's those family/ancestral altars calling to you, suggesting to you, telling you what to do. You may not even be aware that you hear them. They are evil altars, so the devil will send people into your life who further encourage you to do the stuff that is emanating from your family altar. Smoke? Vape? Drink? Illicit Sex? Eat. It's the usual stuff, the usual vices that trap a man in the cycle of sin. The devil starts early. Lie? Cheat? Steal. Kill? Hoping to program you for a lifetime.

Well, if the sequela to sin is death, how can a person start sinning at age 10 and still live to be 100 years old? The devil can keep folks alive who are serving his purposes, especially if no one is paying attention to them. If that evil person is flying under the radar—so to speak--, not God's radar, God sees everything. But if and evil person is so good at being *occultic* and no Christian with a mouth to speak, ears to hear and eyes to see ever sees what this demon-inspired dude is doing and calls judgment on the powers that are operating through him, the devil will seem to be getting away with his schemes through this man.

Could this be the reason there is so much evil in the world? So much evil that needs to be pulled down, but is anyone doing that? *Are you?*

Multiple Altars

It could take a while, sometimes, to SEE what is coming against you. It's why a lot of Christians think that every thing is nice and wonderful. Maybe in the natural. Amen to that if that is the case. But God has been teaching my hands to war and I believe everyone has a measure of warfare to learn and to do. Else, there'd be no reason to provide the spiritual armor of Ephesians 6.

To be able to see what is coming at you in the spirit, especially from occultic folks whose whole goal is to remain hidden so they can manipulate and do whatever they want to others --, that's a little harder.

It took me years to see that I had a spiritual stalker--, dude is seriously obsessed, and I didn't recognize it for the longest, and it was no compliment, and it was not a blessing to me at all --, quite the opposite. I share on that in my book, **BLINDSIDED: Has the Old Man Bewitched You?**

So, on top of satanic altars, there are witchcraft altars coming at folks and they wonder why their life is jacked up.

But if any person breaks free of that altar, if he or she gets saved, and serves God--, God will **keep** him, God will deliver, God will give him or her salvation and bring them into the Kingdom of Heaven, and they shall be saved.

Smile In Your Face

Behold, I send you forth as sheep in the midst of wolves. Be ye therefore wise as serpents and harmless as doves.

But beware of men, for they will deliver you up to the councils, and they will scourge you in their synagogues, (Matthew 10:15-16)

    A guy in a black leotard and a red pitchfork is not going to show up to tempt you. PEOPLE will be the way anything happens in our lives. People will be used.

    But we need people. Yes, we do; no man is an island. There are genuinely nice people and there are real people. There are pretty people, handsome people, fun people, smart people, rich people, and friendly people--, well, at least, at first. Oh, and especially relatives, they are the closest, and have the easiest access to you, so they can be used by the devil. Sorry. But this is where household witchcraft comes from--, people in your household.

There are church people—everyone at church is not saved and everyone at church is not of God. Discern every *spirit*. Note how the above verse warns us to watch out for folks in synagogues (churches). Be wise and discerning. In a church is where the old man from **BLINDSIDED** was situated. So I believed he was a real church man.

Nope; he was not. It took me years --, don't let that be you.

People who smile in your face, but all the while they want to take your place, the backstabbers. Secular music is riddled with descriptions of them, if we would but listen. I'm not recommending secular music, but I'm saying that the WORLD tells on itself, and if you happen to still be listening to that music, then listen, really listen. Let him with ears to hear, hear what the Spirit is saying today.

I used to know a guy, I thought he was a man of God and all about God. Not so.

I used to know a lady who was the most rebuking lady I ever met in my life. Many times, what we need to SEE is right in front of us. Pray the Lord for eyes to SEE what needs to be seen. For example, as it pertains to this rebuking lady --, you'd better know what an evil altar is if you go to someone's house.

God is talking to all of us, if we would but listen. He will show you dangers, tricksters, liars, even household witches. He will show you saboteurs well before it happens, in the dream. If you have a dream of someone impersonating you, know that they are probably **trying to be you, become you, or take something that you have**. I had a dream of a staff person wearing a red evening gown; she walked about the office, then quickly ducked into a room. In the dream I don't think she was supposed to have been seen. The evening gown was identified as mine, in the dream, although I'd never seen it before. Further, it was wrinkled beyond wrinkles--, so she wasn't even doing it well. That was someone who aspired to be me or take my place. Nothing to laugh at, that takes prayer treatment.

Pray about your dreams as soon as you wake up. Handle things in the spirit, immediately.

Subsequently that girl lost her job, and I lost connection with her. **FAILED ASSIGNMENT**: she not only did not become me, but being focused on me and my life, she did not become herself, either.

You cannot know for sure, unless you ask God what any dream means, and exactly what He is trying to impart to you. Ask Him; He will tell you.

Surely, He Has Rejected Me

I've heard more times than one, from God, through the Holy Spirit – **Surely, he has rejected Me**. Or, **Can't you see that he has rejected Me?** Even, **He hasn't rejected you, he has rejected Me**.

Those are the people that we love, loved, or wanted to love, but their agenda was totally different. Their agenda was based on the *god* or *gods* that they serve--, the ones that are in their soul that give them ideas, inclinations, instruction, direction, and programming. If they have rejected God, what do you expect to do with them?

You may wonder, when they do something that hurts you, or your relationship, or life--, why did they do that? They don't know, they've been programmed or instructed. **Evil doesn't**

make sense; it is just evil. Many times, the thing the evil person wants to steal from you, they could just ask you and you'd give it to them. So why did they just do that, that, or *that*? They don't know. It was probably just evil programming.

You know this is evil programming because as soon as one is cast down, struck down, sent away, like a game of Whack-A-Mole, another one pops up, exactly like the last one. Yet, another.

Well, you need to consider your own foundation – are you attracting the same stuff over and over? Then pray for the Lord to cleanse and heal your foundation.

Either way, before or after you pray foundational prayers, you get weary; of course, one can get tired and fatigued. It is not your imagination; it is not paranoia. It is a demonic onslaught.

Whatever the reason it is coming at you, let the Lord teach your hands to war, and do warfare against the attacks of the enemies. Remember, not against flesh and blood even though a physical manifestation may have been what got your attention. As always if you can nip these assaults in the bud at the spirit level, clean up is so much easier.

Why Is This Happening?

Why are these attacks happening to you? Iniquity?--, .yours, ancestral, foundational? Or, maybe none of that, the devil just hates you – who you are in the Spirit. A person that you don't even know yet, the grown up mature person that God designed you to be, that you haven't even seen yet --, is who he hates. The devil hates who you are in the Spirit, and like Herod, wants to strike you out, or strike you down. We are not Jesus, but Herod was after Jesus and He hadn't done anything; he was just *born.*

They, whoever *they* are, say that imitation is the sincerest form of flattery. In high school there was a girl that rode the same school bus that I rode. She never spoke to me, even though, at first, I would speak to her when she got on the bus in the mornings several stops after mine. My mother engrained in all of us to have manners, you greet people when you enter a room, and you speak when spoken to. I added to that to be friendly to people because the Bible says if you want friends, show yourself friendly.

Okay, so I'm a girl in high school who would after doing homework would spend hours creating elaborate braided hairdo's for school the next morning. I'd wrap it or put on a bonnet, and this would save me lots of time the next morning. So, I'd be sitting on the bus all happy and bright on Monday morning in my new hairdo that I had created Sunday night. The non-speaking girl would get on the bus, practically roll her eyes at me. Tuesday, she would have my Monday hairstyle, copied to the tee. I got wise. I changed my hair braiding EVERY night, a day later, whatever I wore she would have it copied exactly.

Maybe you can tell me where the flattery is in that, I've never seen it. In all of high school and thereafter we have never had a conversation and she has never spoken to me. She was a year younger than me, so I had no anger toward her, I just figured she didn't have a clue as to what to do with her hair, which by the way was gorgeous.

Do you think I've ever told anyone this? Of course not. Who would believe it?

The Assignment

If Herod--, that is, the Herodian *spirit* was willing to kill ALL the male babies two years and under in Bethlehem, shall it not stand to reason that especially if you are a baby Christian, been saved for 1 year or 2 years, that you are an automatic candidate for that evil *spirit*. Therefore, once you set your hands to the plow, do not turn back.

But Jesus told him, "Anyone who puts a hand to the plow and then looks back is not fit for the Kingdom of God."

(Luke 9:62 NLT)

Do you know of anyone who would be walking *forward* but their head is turned in a backward direction? It's impossible, but if they are even trying to do that we must ask, are they not sure? Are they not sure of where they are going, what they want to do, or where they have been? Are they not proceeding with their whole heart? Halfheartedly? They are likely to trip or fall. It's impossible to have your head turned to the back, if you are moving forward.

If you are moving forward in God, you keep your eyes on God anyway, not just on any random thing in your path, or future. I look *past* the hills, from whence cometh my help. My help comes from the Lord, the Maker of Heaven and Earth.

The assignment is to steal, kill and destroy. The devil wants to stop the plan of God, but the plan of God is working through God's people in the Earth. The plan of God is working through billions of people. Now, we see why demonic attacks are so widespread.

The devil uses people, too. Without a body no *spirit* has authority on Earth. Yet, there are so many people who believe they can employ the power that the devil has for their own personal gain. Humans who want riches, fame, power, and other things, believe they can *take* from the devil and do what they want. They can't. They won't. Many are deceived, thinking that they are deploying "free energy" that is out here and that they are so smart that they are commanding it to do their bidding. Seems that way, at first. But these are demons. The deceived will find out, either sooner or later --, depends on the devil's purposes.

Yes, I'm saying the blessings of the Lord maketh rich and He adds no sorrow.

But, use of the devil may or may not make rich and it is **full of sorrow**. So watch where you're going. Keep your eyes on God, not on counterfeit promises of the Evil One. Let go of the past and its soul ties and evil covenants before you were saved and delivered. Press forward to the mark of the high calling in Jesus Christ.

Lot's wife got stopped in her tracks, literally. As, and because she was looking back, she turned into a pillar of salt. Not a mound of salt, not a mountain of salt, but a pillar of salt. Pillars are often monuments – perhaps the Lord wanted that to be a memorial to all who turn back to their previous lifestyle, or are drawn back into it, or forced into it – the pillar marks the spot. Some are pulled back into it by their blood and the altars of their father's house. Even after salvation, if you do not get deliverance, you may be subject to every evil, every sin, and every temptation that tempted or ruined your father or mother.

Lot reached the village just as the sun was rising over the horizon. Then the LORD rained down fire and burning sulfur from the sky on Sodom and Gomorrah. He utterly destroyed them, along with the other cities and villages of the plain, wiping out all the people and every bit of vegetation. But Lot's wife looked back as she was following behind him, and she turned into a pillar of salt.

The body is composed of about 250 grams, or a little over a ½ pound of salt. We are 70% water, so the result of a human body being instantly incinerated may leave ashes, but that water evaporates, and the salt remains. The New Testament tells us that we are the salt of the Earth, we are the taste and the seasoning... if it loses it's savor it will be like sand and good for nothing, but to be tread upon.

To me, Lot's wife still had goodness and savor in her. She may have still had ministry and giftings in her for her family, generation, and mankind. When her life was taken away from her because of her love of the world--, the worldliness of Sodom and Gomorrah, the evidence of that salt says that she died by disobedience, and, prematurely.

She still had *salt*.

Don't let that be you.

Be Aware

PRAY to the Lord that He always makes you aware of enemy attacks, witchcraft arrows – not to be oblivious but not to be paranoid either.

Pray to the Lord to make you aware by dreams or signs, or Word of knowledge that you are under attack and what to do about it. Better, pray to know **before** it happens, so you can circumvent disasters. To walk circumspectly means being aware of what is going on around you, yes. But we need to be aware of what is going on with our spiritual body as well as our physical body.

Most often this is what our dreams are to do for us. Don't ignore your dreams. Record them, pray to the Holy Spirit about them. Get correct Christian interpretation of every dream and pray accordingly.

Samson was clueless. It was as though he was blinded by the tricks of Delilah. Samson was probably up late every night with Delilah, cavorting, and courting. If they had cell phones, he and Delilah would have been texting and sexting all day. He was probably totally off his circadian sleep cycle--, exhilarated, but exhausted. In that state he may not have slept enough to even dream. Or, his dreams which most likely were warnings from God--, could have been wiped.

I'm pretty sure he wasn't listening to his parents who may have said, *"Boy, you're taking this Delilah thing too far."* Surely, he wasn't following the precepts of God, else he would not have been fornicating with the seductress. And there was no one with a Word of Wisdom, no report that a Prophet came across his path to warn him, saying, *Dude, this is all too much.*

Samson ignored every possible protection that God puts in place to help man.

Samson died with his enemy.

Naboth didn't realize that he was under attack, and from the witch of all witches, Jezebel, herself. Ahab had asked nicely to buy the vineyard that was adjacent to his. Naboth wouldn't and said he couldn't sell it because it was an inheritance. Jezebel wasn't so nice, as to ask, as we all know.

Saul was after David. Absalom blindsided David. David – were you paying attention, or chasing ladies?

Solomon fell right into the enemy's idolatrous plan, even though God told him, God warned him.

The man in the ditch that was robbed and beaten and left for dead in the synoptic Gospels was not aware that would happen to him, else he might not have gone alone, or that way, at all. Pray you don't miss God at the forewarning stage. Pray God will keep the enemy from doing his worst to you.

Pray the Lord will always send help from Zion, even if you miss it.

IYKYK

If you know, you know.

Hannah knew that sister-wife, Peninnah was up to no good. She did not deceive herself by justifying Peninnah's behavior as, *Oh, that's just the way she is.* Hannah went to the temple and prayed. Hard.

Jesus knew that Judas was after Him, it was the plan of God, after all, Jesus was spiritually woke from Day One. Pharisees, Sadducees, Herod, Sanhedrin Council, Nicolaitans, anyone else? Yeah, pretty much everyone else except those who were standing in line for healing and blessings. Hey, maybe some of those too, since all through the Bible we see how people too quickly forget what God has done for them, and turn away from God, and back to sin, like they are daft or something.

Three wisemen knew not to go back by the way of Herod, as much for themselves as well as for the sake of the baby Jesus. All the folks that God told to go a place or do a thing, but go back by another way, God was letting them know in the spirit before disaster struck in the natural. This is why we must read the Word, pray, praise, worship and seek Facetime with God, the presence of God so He can tell us things we need to know to have a successful life.

We CAN Do This

Knowledge of what has happened, what is happening in real time as well as knowledge of future events, are blessings from God. There's a lot going on, there is no time to play.

So, knowledge of what is happening to your spirit, soul and body and knowledge of past, present, and future are all needed. The reason we have to know all of that is because this life and this demonic warfare is complicated. We also are **responsible** to know it because we **CAN** actually do all that.

> I will praise thee; for I am fearfully and wonderfully made: marvellous are thy works; and that my soul knoweth right well., (Psalm 139:14).

To turn off any one portion of that is worse than never turning on the abilities to do it at all. It is the same as putting the hand to the plow, and then turning back. For whatever reason a person may not progress, freeze in their tracks, or try to regress, like Lot's wife --, because of lack of courage, fear, laziness, worldly cares, love of the world, soul ties, ignorance, being overrun with *spirits* that are not of God, ostrich behavior, turning back from the plow, from the gifts and callings of God is never profitable.

We **CAN** actually do all of that *with* the Holy Spirit, else God would not require it of us. We can only barely monitor our own flesh without the Holy Spirit. The carnal man is so flesh-minded, and now focused that he is not spiritual at all.

Spiritual things are foolishness to him. We are complex beings. To remain only a carnal creature, a flesh being when we have all the hard and software on board to be so much more is as if we choose to remain in kindergarten all of our lives., when there is quantum spiritual stuff to do in the Kingdom of God and by the Grace of the Holy Spirit.

But, because we are God's and created in such a way that we can do all things through Christ which strengthens us, It behooves us to find out if not what those **all things** are, at least find out what some or most of those things are.

I Can Do All Things

I do not think I'm arrogant about what I do or what I can do. I can do all things **through Christ** which strengthens me. *Can't we all?*

I do not know how fine the line is between arrogance and confidence, but I suppose to the unconfident, the unsaved, and those who are not walking in purpose, it must be a very thin line, when judging others. Those of us, in Christ have the Wisdom to know that it is not I that doeth the work, but the Spirit in me that doeth the works, (John 14:10)

No matter what the unsaved or the unfilled say to you, do not come down from the wall that you are building as the Lord has assigned, empowered, and emboldened you to build. Obey God.

> **I can do all things through Christ** which strengtheneth me. (Philippians 4:13)

I have been professing that for more than 20 years, so is it not about time that it *"took"* in my life? Well, amen. I don't much talk about it, I just **do it**. I do as many of those *all things* as I can, the Good Lord willing.

Jesus thought it not robbery to be equal with God. I do not think it to be robbery or arrogance to believe a Scripture verse that is actually about me. Faith is. Faith is now. Faith pleases God.

> Who, being in the form of **God, thought it not robbery** to be equal with **God:** · But made himself of no reputation, and took upon him the form of a servant, (Philippians 2:6)

Saints of God, it is not robbery to appropriate a Scripture verse for your life and to use Faith to do what that Verse says you can do. Amen.

I have met more folks, carnal or Christian, in or out of the Church, than I care to name, who want to figure me out, do what I do, do things the way I do them. *Become* me. Try to be me better than I'm being myself. Sad, really because that means the self that they are supposed to be is not going to be available in the Earth. They themselves will not be in place to do the things that God has placed, ordained, gifted them to do, while they try to be a cheap copy of someone else.

Years ago, as a teen, as we were listening to a popular singer on the radio, I said to my brother, *I can sing just like that.*

He, drily said to me. *Why? They already have someone to sing like her, why would they want another one?*

Words to live by.

You do not need someone to be you better than you are being yourself. Not when we all have been created as masterpieces and designer originals. Your DNA, your temperament, personality, natural and spiritual giftsets are a totally unique combination. Even if you have an identical twin, are you two, indeed, identical? I'll answer that by Jacob and Esau who were fraternal based on their descriptions. But God said He loved one and hated the other. So, even twins are not the SAME to God, so you know you are not able to become someone else because you admire them or are jealous of them, or think you *love* them.

I say all this because that is the motive and the thought process inspired into many evil human agents against folks like you or me. It is ungodly thought, even though it is provocative and causes too many to jump into action – in their flesh. Flesh works can be successful, but if you are in God and someone is coming at you in the flesh, go ahead and stamp that file: **FAILED ASSIGNMENT**. Rock, paper, scissors—doesn't matter, SPIRIT will win out over flesh every time.

    I have met more than 5 sets of identical twins in person. They look different to me; I can always tell the difference. One seems to be an introvert, the other is the extrovert. Have you noticed, similarly? Even on TV identical twins, in all that makeup, still look different.

    People who are in competition with you, and you have absolutely no knowledge that they are competing with you will try almost anything, even evil exchange and masquerades. Be wise, be discerning, stay prayed up. Always.

Friends Are Rare

Henceforth I call you not servants; for the servant knoweth not what his lord doeth: but I have called you friends; for all things that I have heard of my Father I have made known unto you.

Ye have not chosen me, but I have chosen you, and ordained you, that ye should go and bring forth fruit, and that your fruit should remain: that whatsoever ye shall ask of the Father in my name, he may give it you.

John 15:15-16

Friends are rare. If you find one, cherish him or her. If you have one, you are blessed indeed. Most I have met have ended up in other categories.

Once, I introduced a girlfriend to my brother at a dinner party with my husband, so the four of us had a really nice dinner that I cooked. She spent more time looking through my house and asking me ridiculous questions such as whose was this when you two met and got married? Was this yours or his? Really? These questions applied to everything that she felt like asking about, even the houseplants.

Hey, whatever, I'm thinking she's just rude or tacky, but if she and my brother hit it off, then it's not going to be a problem, since she's already my "friend." She and my brother did not hit it off, but the next day when I spoke to her over the phone, she told me that I was *"Over there living the life that she wanted."* She said I was living *"her life."*

The Blood of Jesus is against that covetous word curse.

In interpersonal relationships, I've dated fellows for months and into years, then one day they believe they have me figured out, and they can do what I do – whatever that thing is. You see, with the ministry of Helps, you--, any and all of us, by the Holy Spirit can arise to many occasions and fulfill many needs and help many people.

You can supply a need or support for others, but without the right Spirit in them, they end up resenting you for helping them, or they feel shame because they needed you. Once some of these folks believe they can now do what you do they no longer "need" you. They got this. Please know, the Holy Spirit is not a quick study. The way gifts work in and through me, is uniquely of God and cannot be duplicated.

Respectfully, I say the same applies to you. You are a designer original with gifts, abilities, and administration of those gifts like no other person on this Earth. Give God the Glory!

The most telling of these things was that before the break up the individual would attempt to dismantle me or tear me down, and then after the breakup would try to mimic what I did for them in their life. They would usually fail miserably.

So what is this?

It's a **FAILED ASSIGNMENT.**

It was someone trying to steal virtue, gifts, skills, and talents. And failing at it. What God gave you is yours, and as long as you stay in proper relationship and position with God, He will not let anyone rip you off, although the devil may send one and then another against you.

When stealing or exchanging doesn't work, their next best attempt is to try to mimic another's virtues, gifts, skills, and talents. Of course, in the natural, many will try to copy your hairstyle and style of dress. (It gets so old, doesn't it?) They'll fail at that, too. There is only one real you. There is only one real me.

Thank God for protection, spiritual protection, in Jesus' Name, amen.

Because of whose you are, folks will want to make alliances and covenant with you. The Gibeonites made covenant with the Israelites by hook and crook. They lied as to their identity. Beware of wolves pretending to be sheep, and *friends*.

But when God blesses you with a **real** friend or friends, thank God and hold dear your friend.

Pharisees

Pharisees followed Jesus along with the multitude to try to entrap Him--, ***as if.*** My niece says to me often, "Of all the people in the world, they picked you? You? They picked you to try to outsmart or get over on?"

Well.

Of all the people the Pharisees decided to try to undo--, they picked Jesus? The Son of God? Are they daft?

Possibly, but mostly they are demonically programmed. And look, those are the folks that were running the synagogue. If they are trying to **kill** the person they should be worshipping, can we surmise that they may be worshipping the person that they should be getting out of their presence and out of their lives?

Pharisees asked Him hard questions…. Those passages are listed below, but I want us to consider that no where in the Bible do we see that the Pharisees, or any other *religious* person asked the devil any hard question. Why not? When folks are deceived, they celebrate the one they should not and they interrogate and castigate the one they should be celebrating.

Jesus and God both asked Satan whatever they wanted to know. In Job, God asked the devil, **Where have you been?** In the NT, Jesus spoke directly to the devil as well.

These carnal Pharisees, although they thought themselves holy did the opposite of what Holy men should do. The Word says that we shall know folks by their fruit. So there's that.

Then went the Pharisees, and took counsel how they might entangle him in his talk. And they sent out unto him their disciples with the Herodians, saying, Master, we know that thou art true, and teachest the way of God in truth, neither carest thou for any man: for thou regardest not the person of men. Tell us therefore, What thinkest thou? Is it lawful to give tribute unto Cesar, or not?

But Jesus perceived their wickedness, and said, Why tempt ye me, ye hypocrites? Shew me the tribute money. And they brought unto him a penny. And he saith unto them, Whose is this image and superscription? They say unto him, Cesar's. then saith he unto them, Render therefore unto Cesar the things which are Cesar's and unto God the things that are God's. When they had heard these *words*, they marvelled, and left him, and went their way, *(Matthew 22:15-22)*

Jesus perceived their wickedness. He discerned it. He peeped their motives and answered accordingly. We should do the same, using our spiritual gifts for our own protection and to guard both the Word and our ministries.

Read the rest of the Chapter in Matthew to see the relentless nature of the devil. Question after question they threw at Jesus to try to trap Him in His knowledge of the Scripture, as if they are smarter than God. Smarter than the Son of God.

You too, are supposed to be a son of God, so study to show yourself approved, so when decisions and hard questions come, you will answer by the Word and in Truth.

Even If A Tree

Don't be dismayed if you did fall into a trap, or adversity. Don't be downcast if you fell for a fake friend or fellow. Even if a tree is cut down, at the sound of water, it shall live again.

For there is hope of a tree, if it be cut down, that it will sprout again, and that the tender branch thereof will not cease. (Job 14:7)

Jesus was cut down, but He is resurrected; He lives!

Even if every assignment sent against you by the devil has not failed and some evil arrows hit, some arrows of affliction did not miss, you are still vertical today, praise God! While there is life, there is hope. The spirit of a man sustains him in times of trouble. This is one of the reasons we should always be in prayer and the Word, to build up our spirit man so we can endure in Seasons of War or affliction.

If God can use a thing, He will allow a thing, especially things that grow us up and increase our faith and teach our hands to war. Grape vines, for example, that grow in certain regions of France, grow on very stony ground and they are not allowed to be watered. Only God can water them. Those plants then become very hardy. You, if God is only watering you, then you will be sure to get the right stuff, the right nutrients, in the right seasons, for your edification and growth. *As* long as you adhere to God's plan and don't wander off and get doctrine from Lord knows where, all will go well with your life.

God can sustain the man going through strenuous times. God can find he who is lost. God can even resurrect that which appears dead. God can speak and prophesy to dead bones and they will live again. God can breathe life and also new life into any one who is or will be one of His; He desires that not one would be lost.

So before you were in Christ, or even after, if you have fallen into sin, rebellion, or disobedience, do not lose heart. Do not fall into condemnation. Do not be downcast, but repent, renounce the sin, break any evil covenant that was formed.

Put on the whole armor of God and get into spiritual warfare. Bind every demon assigned to enforce any evil covenant against you, and get them out of your life. Break all evil yokes, bondages and pray the Lord to heal your foundation. Rededicate yourself and your life to God and stay in the Word and be instant and constant in prayer.

We all have sinned and fallen short of the Glory of God, but in Him there is no condemnation. Yes, the Holy Spirit convicts us of sin, so we repent, that is we turn from our wicked ways and seek the

Face of God again. God is faithful, merciful, and just to forgive us and cleanse us again, with the Blood of Jesus.

Even if you sin and the Law of Sin and death has been invoked against you, Jesus is your Advocate and the Blood of Jesus is your defense. Yes, you are guilty, say so in the Courts of Heaven and plead the Blood of Jesus. The Lord will forgive, and you will LIVE again. Just a hint, just the scent, the sound of the Living Water from the Throne of Grace will cause the deadness of your life and your tree to live again.

Adam & Eve failed. God slew the Lamb from the foundation of the Earth and redeemed mankind back to Himself.

Moses failed; he still was chosen to bring God's people out of Egyptian bondage.

David failed, he still became a mighty king over Israel.

Jonah failed; yet God sill delivered him out of that ship, and out of that whale and provided shade for him in the smiting son after he was cast ashore.

Saul failed and he became Paul.

Peter failed; Jesus said before the dawn you will deny me thrice, and that is exactly what happened.

Praise God and give Him His glory; if He did it for other humans who failed, He will do it for you. Repent, seek God's face and keep progressing in purpose toward your destiny.

Make Your Boast

Yes, you can do all things through Christ which strengthens you. Make your boast in the Lord. Yes, enjoy your good successes in the Lord. Yes, give your testimony in and out of the sanctuary, but make sure it is a God-focused testimony, else you may appear braggadocious, and you will lose friends and draw enemies.

As the devil answered when God asked him where he had been, he said he had been *to and fro* in the Earth seeking whom he could destroy or devour. Put your business out there on social media or even at work bragging on yourself all your successes, your accomplishments, and holdings, you will draw the wrong stuff to yourself. If the devil is looking to devour someone, don't make it easy for him to find you.

My soul shall make her boast in the LORD: the humble shall hear thereof, and be glad. O magnify the LORD with me, and let us exalt his name together. (Psalm 34:9)

But when you make your boast in the Lord, you put all listening ears on notice, I am in God and He is in me. When you come against me, you come against the Person that I am in covenant with. God will contend with those who contend with me. When you give your overcoming testimony in the sanctuary, you probably include how God has come through for you many times, from teenagerhood to young adulthood, to even now and that He's never lost a battle and He's never failed you. Even when you failed, the Lord pulled you out of your polluted blood and cleaned you up and made you one of His, Amen!

Say No to Woe!

So, drop the *oh woe is me* complaint. God hates murmuring, complaining. If you are prone to that, you will just get more and more of what you are complaining about.

Don't you hate it when you do something nice, or kind, or wonderful for someone and they don't even appreciate it? Your kid – are they never satisfied? God can wonder that about some of us. He keeps us 24/7. He doesn't sleep or slumber, but we do. God is merciful, gracious, kind. He has sent a Helper for us. He gave His Only Begotten Son; He keeps us out of harm's way all day and all night.

The only trouble we really get into is trouble that we walk our own legs into.

The trouble we decide to walk into because of ignorance, disobedience, rebellion.

God is not letting anything just happen to us. Nothing by any means can take us out of the hands of God. He said so, and He is faithful. So we really don't have anything to complain about.

Take the time to meditate on and remember the goodness of God, the protection, the safety that He allows you to dwell in. He gives rest to His beloved. Are you not beloved of God?

Mankind needs to stop acting like God doesn't do anything for us because of there's a thing that we want today or we want something so desperately, that we don't have. No one is amused by tantrums. That thing we may want so badly is usually ungodly, or out of season, if we don't have it. We may not be ready for it. No, we cannot have someone else's life or spouse, or house, or car, or kids, or hair, skin, beauty, job, or money – all that is demonic and covetous.

If you really look at it, there is probably nothing that you have asked God for, or are asking God for that He hasn't given you provided you are walking upright before Him, and at least working on soul prosperity. If God can trust you to have it and it won't interfere with your purpose and destiny, He will give it to you.

He probably has already given it to you--, He may just be waiting for you to make yourself **ready** to receive it.

God is spending His time, energy and effort protecting you and God is amazing at everything He does. If demonic onslaughts, fake friends, and enemies are coming up against you –, that's probably not on God--, it's on you. We all must look at our inner life to see what we either did to cause it, or what our ancestors did to cause it.

Is it random because we are so wonderful – *oh pls.* Is it a prophetic attack because of who we are supposed to grow into, *in God*?

Were we disobedient and fell under judgment with God? No curse can alight without a cause.

Still, in His Mercy even if we were wrong, but we quickly repent, God will help us out of the messes we make in our own lives. Wouldn't you do that for your own children?

So, in tandem with looking at all the times God has helped you, kept you, protected you, and delivered you, you must add in repentance, because God didn't just let the devil attack you. There was cause in there, either yours or through your foundation and ancestors. All this was a wakeup call for you to get into prayer regarding your ancestry, your foundation to get it healed. All these skirmishes, battles and wars were not just to trouble you and irritate your life, they were wake up calls for you to arise and do some spiritual work in your life. Do it, for the sake of your own generations that God may be well-pleased with you and your bloodline.

What This Means

"Trouble don't last always."

God will bring you through these troubles and into a season of rest. Pray God that it is a perpetual season, but that there is rest, indeed.

When a devil agent or entity fails, there is no mercy for them with the devil.

Once you are made aware of the enemy's plan against you and you do something about it, you can proclaim **FAILED ASSIGNMENT** against that enemy. Also, by our authority, and God-given power your declaration of **FAILED ASSIGNMENT** can get you at least two things that are no small things. You may send that enemy to the Pit for early torment, to the Pit where there is no water, and there is no return.

> "What do you want with us, Son of God?" they shouted. "Have you come here to torture us before the appointed time?"
> (Matthew 8:29)

Once found out and the warfare is done, and we will win--, this enemy is banned from your life forever. All sons of God (that should be us, too) have the authority to cast out demons. As Jesus was casting out devils they knew where they would be going – for early torment. Why? Because they had been found out early.

The enemy you see this day, you shall see them no more!

> And Moses said unto the people, Fear ye not, stand still, and see the salvation of the LORD, which he will shew to you to day: for the Egyptians whom ye have seen to day, ye shall see them again no more for ever.
> (Exodus 14:13)

If you are seeing them no more, then where are they going?

And since you have spoiled, ruined, or defeated this enemy, you can now receive **spoil** or **spoils** for being victorious in battle and war. That is always the case with God. To the victor, go the spoils.

The enemy has to give back to you seven times (7X) what was stolen, taken, withheld, kept away from you because you found him out and you defeated him.

7X.

Go get it. Get into that warfare, possess your possessions, get the things that pertain to your peace and win back and win even more spoils for the trouble that you've been through. God is a God of balance – the enemy must pay, even if it depletes his store.

Take your victory lap. Enter into your Peace and get back all that was stolen from you.

Give God the Glory Amen.

Dear Reader

Thank you for acquiring and reading this book. I pray that it has enlightened and strengthened you.

May the Lord break you out of every captivity and may He restore you *at least* sevenfold, all that you have lost and all that has been taken from you. Even ***time,*** as He restores the years. In the Name of Jesus, Amen.

Dr. Marlene Miles

Other books by this author

AK: The Adventures of the Agape Kid

AMONG SOME THIEVES

Ancestral Powers

Blindsided: *Has the Old Man Bewitched You?*

https://a.co/d/5O2fLLR

Churchzilla, The Wanna-Be, Supposed-to-be Bride of Christ

Demons Hate Questions

Devil Weapons: Unforgiveness, Bitterness,…

Dream Defilement

Don't Refuse Me, Lord (4 book series)

Every Evil Bird

Evil Touch

Fantasy Spirit Spouse

FAT Demons (The): *Breaking Demonic Curses*

The Fold (4 book series)

The Fold (Book 1)

Name Your Seed (Book 2)

The Poor Attitudes of Money (3)

Do Not Orphan Your Seed got HEALING? Verses for Life got LOVE? Verses for Life got HOPE? Verses for Life got money?

How to Dental Assist

Let Me Have A Dollar's Worth

Living for the NOW of God

Lose My Location https://a.co/d/crD6mV9

Man Safari, *The*

Marriage Ed. Rules of Engagement & Marriage

Made Perfect in Love

Motherboard (The) - soul prosperity series

Plantation Souls

Power Money: Nine Times the Tithe

The Power of Wealth *(forthcoming)*

Rules of Engagement & Marriage

Seasons of Grief

Seasons of War

Soul Prosperity soul prosperity series 3

https://a.co/d/5p8YvCN

Souls Captivity soul prosperity series 2

The Spirit of Poverty

This Is NOT That: How to Keep Demons from Coming At You

Throne of Grace: Courtroom Prayer

Time Is of the Essence

Too Many Wives: *Why You Have Lady Problems*

Tormenting Spirits   https://a.co/d/dAogEJf

Triangular Power *(series)*

    Powers Above

    SUNBLOCK

    Do Not Swear by the Moon

    STARSTRUCK

Upgrade: How to Get Out of Survival Mode

Toxic Souls (Book 2 of series)

Legacy (Book 3 of series)

Warfare Prayer Against Beauty Curses Warfare Prayer Against Poverty

When the Devourer is Rebuked

The Wilderness Romance *(series)*

- *The Social Wilderness*
- *The Sexual Wilderness*
- *The Spiritual Wilderness*

Images adapted from: Fiery Icarus
Illustration 291465009 © Cary Peterson | Dreamstime.com

And Movie Shootout ID145381545 © Christos Georghiou
|Dreamstime.com